THE HOBBIT™

AN UNEXPECTED JOURNEY

The Movie Storybook

"In a hole in the ground, there lived a hobbit..."

First U.S. edition

Text by Paddy Kempshall
First published by HarperCollins *Children's Books* in 2012

For information about permission to reproduce selections from this book, write to Permissions, Houghton Mifflin
Harcourt Publishing Company, 215 Park Avenue South, New York, New York 10003.

www.hmhbooks.com

Library of Congress Cataloging-in-Publication Data is available.
ISBN 978-0-547-89872-8

Printed in the United States
HC 10 9 8 7 6 5 4 3 2 1

THE HOBBIT™

AN UNEXPECTED JOURNEY

The Movie Storybook

Houghton Mifflin Harcourt
Boston   New York
2012

The Lonely Mountain, or Erebor, was once the legendary home of the Dwarven Kings and a place of riches. That was until the arrival of a great dragon called Smaug. In a fury of fire and blood, Smaug drove the Dwarven King from his home and scattered his people to the farthest parts of Middle-earth.

The Lonely Mountain became Smaug's lair. While people secretly hoped for the glorious return of the King, there were few brave enough to try to wrest control of Erebor from its evil resident. Until now...

One fine morning in the Shire, Bilbo Baggins is sitting outside his home at Bag End after a delightful breakfast. He is approached by an old man, dressed from head to toe in grey, with a pointed hat and a large staff.

This strange person is the legendary Wizard Gandalf the Grey, who wants him to share in an adventure!

"We don't want any adventures here, thank you," says Bilbo, politely. "Not today."

With that, he hurries back inside his hobbit-hole and thinks no more of it.

Outside, chuckling to himself, Gandalf approaches the round, green door of Bilbo's house and carves into it a strange symbol with his staff...

The following day there is a loud knock at Bilbo's door. Opening the door, Bilbo is surprised to find a large, hairy Dwarf!

"Dwalin at your service," rumbles the Dwarf as he walks past Bilbo.

Before Bilbo can work out what is happening, there is another knock at the door. This time it is another Dwarf, called Balin!

With another knock, two more Dwarves arrive and introduce themselves as Fili and Kili. Just when Bilbo thinks that is that, there is another knock at the door. This time he is extremely surprised to see eight more Dwarves: Oin, Gloin, Ori, Dori, Nori, Bofur, Bombur and Bifur – as well as Gandalf!

"We appear to be one Dwarf short," says the Wizard, entering the hallway.
Poor Bilbo is quite flustered. Suddenly there is another loud bang on the door and in walks a very important-looking Dwarf.

"Allow me to introduce the leader of our Company – Thorin Oakenshield," says Gandalf.

Thorin explains that he is the rightful heir to Erebor, the Lonely Mountain, and is on a quest to reclaim his kingdom. All Thorin needs is a skilled burglar to help, and Gandalf has told him that Bilbo is just the hobbit for the job! Bilbo can't believe it!

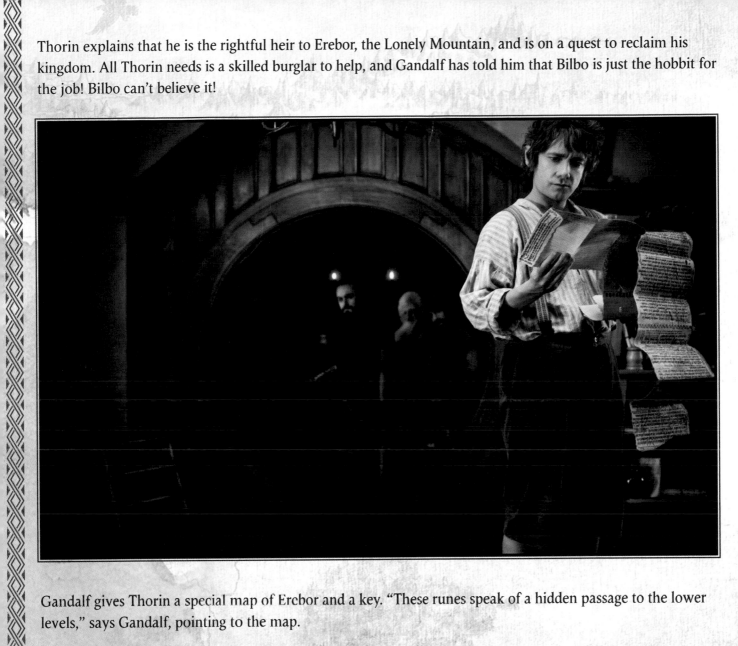

Gandalf gives Thorin a special map of Erebor and a key. "These runes speak of a hidden passage to the lower levels," says Gandalf, pointing to the map.

East lie the Iron hills where is Dain

The Lonely Mountain

Here was Girion Lord in Dale

Here was Thror King under the Mountain

Ravenhill

The Running River

Here is the gateway of the Long Lake

Later that night, Bilbo tries to tell Gandalf that these sort of grand, unexpected adventures are really not his kind of thing.

"Can you promise me that I'll come back?" Bilbo asks Gandalf, uneasily. "No," Gandalf replies darkly. "And even if you do, you will not be the same."

The next morning, when Bilbo wakes, without thinking he rushes out of his home at Bag End and off on a very unexpected adventure!

On their journey Gandalf tells Bilbo about his fellow wizard, Radagast, who lives beyond the Misty Mountains in Mirkwood Forest and loves all plants and animals. Radagast discovered there is a terrible sickness in the forest and has told Gandalf about it.

At the Company's camp, Fili and Kili are looking after the ponies when they notice that some of them have gone missing.

As official burglar, Bilbo is asked to investigate, so he creeps off into the dark forest with Fili and Kili. In the gloom, they peer over a fallen log and discover a strange light. As they draw closer, they see three Trolls huddled around a fire. The Trolls have stolen the ponies and are going to eat them for their supper!

Creeping quietly into the Trolls' camp, Bilbo tries desperately to untie the ponies, but the knots are too tight. Just then he notices that one of the Trolls has a stone knife hanging from his belt. He tries to steal the knife, but he isn't as good a burglar as everyone thinks he is and he gets caught!

Seeing that their friend is in danger, Fili and Kili rush from the trees and attack. Soon Thorin and the rest of the Dwarves arrive and, swinging their axes and hammers, they bravely join the battle. As the Dwarves fight the Trolls, Bilbo manages to sneak away and free the ponies.

As brave and strong as the Dwarves are, the Trolls are stronger and soon the Dwarves are captured!

Stuffed into sacks, Bilbo and his friends can only wait while the Trolls decide how they are going to cook their latest tasty prizes.

Just as things are looking very bleak, the Trolls start to argue with each other. In fact they argue so much that they don't realise that it is getting light.

With a shout, Gandalf suddenly appears on top of a nearby rock. He smashes his staff into the rock beneath his feet. As the rock cracks, the first rays of dawn spill through the hole and splash the Trolls with sunlight, turning them to stone!

Knowing that the Trolls must have had a hideout nearby, Thorin and Gandalf start to search. Soon they discover a hidden cave. They find three amazing swords and it is clear that these weapons are something special. Gandalf, Thorin and Bilbo take one of the swords each, and press on with their journey.

As they leave the cave the group hear a terrible sound – they are being hunted by ferocious Wargs! Howling and gnashing their jaws, two of the enormous beasts come crashing out of the trees, ridden by bloodthirsty Orcs.

"Arm yourselves," cries Gandalf, as the Dwarves once more leap into battle.

Swinging his new sword, Thorin cuts the head off a Warg with one mighty blow and sends it crunching to the ground. Then, taking careful aim, Kili shoots a single arrow fizzing through the air – and straight into the head of the other Warg, killing it instantly.

"We have to get out of here," cries Gandalf. "Follow me."

With Wargs snapping at their heels, Gandalf leads the group through the wilds and into the foothills of the Misty Mountains. As the enemies gain on them, Gandalf hurries the Company into a hidden valley in the rocks just in time.

"Welcome to the Last Homely House East of the Sea," says Gandalf.

Bilbo and his friends have entered Rivendell. Home of the Elves, it is a secret and magical place where the evil Wargs do not dare to follow. However, Dwarves and Elves are not the best of friends and some of the group are not too happy about entering Rivendell.

"Why seek refuge with the enemy – Elves," shudders Gloin in disgust.

But as they enter further into the valley, Bilbo has no such worries. "It feels like magic," he says, amazed by the peace and beauty of the hidden valley.

They are met by the Lord of Rivendell, Elrond. An old friend of Gandalf, Elrond is happy to offer the group a place to rest.

That night, Elrond reveals that Gandalf and Thorin's swords are ancient blades from the Goblin wars called Glamdring and Orcrist. Thorin then shows Elrond his map of the Lonely Mountain. Elrond knows that the strange writing on the map is moon runes.

"Moon runes can only be read by the light of a moon of the same shape and season in which they were written," he tells them.

Luckily for Thorin, that very night is exactly the right time to read the runes! As the rays of the moon shine on the map, Elrond reveals that they describe how to open a secret door into the lair of the dragon!

While everyone else sleeps, Gandalf is called into an important meeting with Elrond, Galadriel and Saruman. As members of the White Council it is their task to ensure that Middle-earth is protected from the forces of wickedness.

"There is something at work beyond the evil of Smaug," says Gandalf. "Something far more powerful..."

While Gandalf is in the meeting, the rest of the group have carried on their journey up into the Misty Mountains.

Taking shelter in a cave, the Company make plans to spend the night in safety.

As Bofur sits at the entrance to the cave, keeping watch, Bilbo huddles up and starts to fall asleep. But just then the floor of the cave drops away, swallowing the group and plunging them into darkness! Tumbling end over end along a dark, damp chute, Bilbo and his friends come clattering to a halt inside a rusty cage. Peering out through the bars, they realise they have been captured by Goblins!

Surrounded by a horde of these slimy, scabby monsters, the Dwarves are led off in a line through the dark tunnels. Bilbo is at the back of the line and suddenly realises that there are no other Goblins behind him! Seizing his chance, he quickly slips off into a gloomy side-tunnel and tries to escape.

Bilbo hasn't made as clean a getaway as he thought, however, and soon finds himself being chased through the caverns by a Goblin. As the slimy, scarred creature gets closer, Bilbo draws his sword and sees that it is glowing with an eerie blue light.

The Goblin pounces, slashing at Bilbo. Struggling and stumbling, Bilbo slips and both he and the Goblin fall headlong into a dark crevasse, plunging even further into the gloom below.

The Goblin is killed in the fall, but Bilbo is now alone and lost.

Scared, Bilbo crawls through the tunnels. He moves forward, warily, through the dark until suddenly his hand finds something lying in the dirt on the floor. It is a plain gold ring. Without thinking, Bilbo pops the ring into his pocket and continues on his way.

As he fumbles along, Bilbo finds his way to the shore of an underground lake. In the middle of the water is a small island and on it is crouched a shrivelled, grey figure.

The small figure on the island spins around, and stares at Bilbo from the darkness with large, yellow eyes.

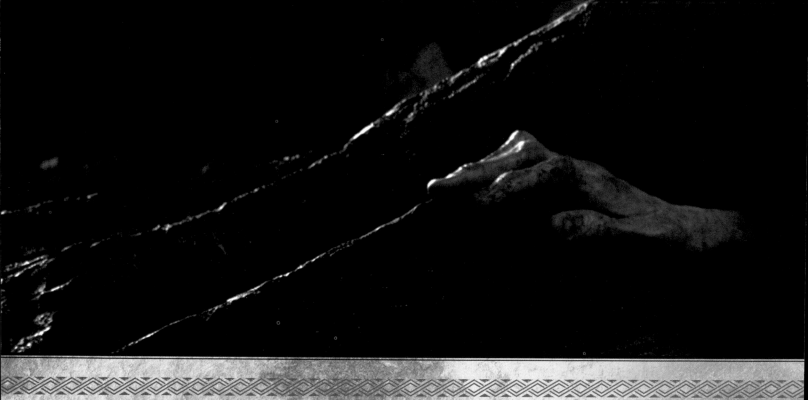

The strange creature is known as Gollum and he has lived in the darkness of the caves for many years.

Bilbo explains that he needs a safe way out, but Gollum won't help for nothing. Instead he challenges Bilbo to a game of riddles – a game with a deadly prize. If Bilbo wins, then Gollum will show him the way out of the caves...

"But if Bagginses loses," smiles Gollum, hungrily, "then we eats it whole!"

Bilbo and Gollum try to outwit each other, but neither of them can think of a riddle that the other can't solve. Eventually, Bilbo thinks of something.

"What have I got in my pocket?" he asks Gollum.

Gollum can't answer and Bilbo has won! But what Bilbo doesn't know is that the ring in his pocket is actually Gollum's prized possession – his precious. Gollum keeps on trying to guess what Bilbo has in his pocket, until he suddenly has a horrible thought – maybe it is his precious ring!

"Curse us and crush us, my precious is lost," wails Gollum. "Thief! Bagginses!"

With a hateful fire in his eyes, Gollum pounces at Bilbo and chases him through the tunnels, trying to get his precious ring back.

While trying to escape, Bilbo stumbles; the ring flies through the air and lands on his finger. It slips on and starts to work its magic.

Meanwhile, Thorin and the Dwarves are pulled deeper and deeper into Goblin Town. The Company are dragged before the Goblin King. A massive creature, he is ugly even by Goblin standards.

Thorin and his friends bravely refuse to reveal any information about their quest – so the Goblin King gives orders for them to be executed.

Just as the Goblin army is about to strike, there is a massive flash of light in the darkness. Gandalf has returned! The Goblins scatter, blinded and confused by the light and the Dwarves seize their chance. Grasping their weapons, they swing into action. But there are far more Goblins than the Dwarves can hope to defeat alone.

"Only one thing can save us," cries Gandalf. "Daylight!"

Swarms of Goblins appear and chase after the Company. As the Goblin King closes in, Gandalf steps forward and draws out the mighty Glamdring.

Gandalf's blade strikes at the heart of the Goblin King, killing him. Their spirits dashed by the death of their King, the Goblins pause. Thorin and his friends take advantage of their enemies' hesitation and race off into the caverns.

Meanwhile, Bilbo is still trying to escape from Gollum. Wearing the ring, Bilbo discovers that he is invisible! Quietly he follows Gollum to the exit of the caves. Then Bilbo leaps over the wretched creature and escapes.

Suddenly Bilbo appears behind the Company. Everyone is happy to be back together, but there is no time to lose. Riding atop their vicious Wargs, Orcs suddenly appear, eager to hunt down the quarry they lost outside Rivendell.

Soon the Company find themselves surrounded. Thinking quickly, Gandalf orders everyone to climb the nearby trees.

Perched among the leaves, Bilbo and his friends look on helplessly as a new, even deadlier enemy arrives. Sitting astride an enormous Warg, the hideous Orc chieftain rides into view.

With one order from the Orc, the Wargs attack. As the mighty beasts hack and bash at the trees below, Gandalf has an idea. Gently catching a moth in his hands, he whispers a secret message to it and sends it off into the darkening skies. Next, he grabs some pine cones and works his magic upon them. Hurled down to the ground, the cones explode in flames, burning everything around them.

Unfortunately for the Company, the trees they are in also catch fire. Soon everyone is huddled in the last tree. Circling below them, the Wargs close in for the kill.

Before the Orcs can deliver the killing strike, a group of giant Eagles sweeps in from the sky. They have received Gandalf's message and have come to rescue everyone. One by one, the Eagles gather up the group with their mighty talons and fly off, leaving the Wargs helpless in the burning forest.

Although rescued and in relative safety, the Company cannot relax. They are only just beginning their journey.

The evil dragon, Smaug, still rules the Lonely Mountain and there is much to be done before Bilbo and his friends can rest. There are far more dangers, excitements and adventures to come on their epic quest.